Last Poems

First published in 1999 by
Slow Dancer Press
91 Yerbury Rd, Londn N19 4RW, England

Published by arrangement with Farrar, Strauss and Giroux Inc.,
19 Union Square West, New York 10003, USA
All rights reserved

British Library Cataloguing-in-Publication Data.
A catalogue record
for this book is available from The British Library.

ISBN 1 871033 51 9

Slow Dancer poetry titles are available in the U.K. through
Signature Book Representation distributed by
Littlehampton Book Services

Cover design: Keenan

Printed by Bell & Bain Ltd, Glasgow

This book is set in Elegant Garamond 10/13

Last Poems

James Schuyler

With an afterword by Lee Harwood

Contents

Mark

My father was ribald
about religion: when
he said, "Did the priest
come riding in on his ass?"

My mother said, "Oh, *Mark*."
Confusing, if you're only four
and everyone else so serious:
mother, her friend who took me

to that big empty box of
a room where all was gray,
empty, ugly: only the priest
and Mabel and me, it seemed.

On that overcast day
a haze like smoke (it
was smoke) moved about,
gray trails in gray Sunday air,

and into me: do you think
I could forget? I did:
just the memory sometimes
of a room like a cold gray box

where I sat beside Mabel,
enrapt, an arrow in my heart.

Horse-Chestnut Trees and Roses

Twenty-some years ago, I read Graham Stuart Thomas's
"Colour in the Winter Garden." I didn't plant
a winter garden, but the book led on to his
rose books: "The Old Shrub Roses," "Shrub Roses
of Today," and the one about climbers and ramblers.

By the corner of the arbor I planted the splendid
Nevada (a Spanish rose, Pedro Dot) and on the arbor
yellow Lawrence Johnston— I've never known
anyone who made a real success of that. Then
a small flowered rose (like a blackberry in flower),
whose name I forget, and then, oh loveliness, oh
glory, Mme. Alfred Carrière, white, with a faintest
blush of pink, and which will bloom even on a
north wall. I used to shave and gaze down into her—
morning kisses. The day Robert Kennedy died, a
green and evil worm crawled out of a bud. I killed
it, a gardening Sirhan Sirhan

At the corner of the house Rosa Mutabilis fluttered
its single, changeable wings. My favorite perhaps.

Then, in the border, along the south side of
the white house, Golden Wings (a patented rose—
did you know you can patent roses? well you can);
prickly, purplish Rose de Rescht; Souvenir
de la Malmaison (named by a Russian Grand Duke in
honor of the Empress Joséphine, Empress of Rosarians);
Mabel Morrison, lifting her blowsy white blooms
to the living room windows.

Then Georg Arends, whose silver-pink petals
uniquely fold into sharp points (or is Georg
my favorite?).

And darkly brooding Prince Camille de Rohan, on
which, out of a cloudless sky, a miraculous rain
once fell. (But I'm forgetting Gloire de Dijon,
Dean Hole's favorite rose.)

Then the smallest, most delicate, delectable
of all, Rose de Meaux. Alas, it pined away.

And elsewhere more: Rosa Gallica, the striped
and the pink, the Pembertons, Persian yellow,
and unforgettable cerise Zéphirine Drouhin.
And a gray rose, Reine des Violettes. Sweet-
brier, Mme. Pierre Oger, Variegata di Bologna,
"like raspberries and cream." and more,
whose names escape me

I went by there Sunday last and they're gone, all
gone, uprooted, supplanted by a hateful "foundation
planting" of dinky conifers, some pointed, some
squatty roundish. I put a curse on it and them.

On either side of the front walk there towered two
old horse-chestnut trees. I loved their sticky,
unfurling leaves, and when they bore their candles
it was magic, breath-catching, eye-delighting. Cut
down, cut down. What kind of man cuts down trees
that took all those years to grow? I do not
understand.

Oh, well, it's his house now, and I remove the
curse, but not without a hope that Rose de Rescht
and the rugosas gave him a good scratching. He
deserved it.

But oh dear: I forgot the five Old China Monthly
roses, and I always wish I'd planted Félicité
et Perpétue—it's their names I like. And
Climbing Lady Hillingdon

(But the Garland grown as a fountain seemed
somehow beyond me.)

There are roses and roses, always more roses,
It's the horse-chestnut trees I mind.

Mood Indigo

for David Trinidad

. . . and the curtain rose in that theatre so long ago
and the music is playing
the first song I fell in
love to today so soon
                is it possible
and there, gigantic, is the face
on the backdrop
of the elegant Duke
              the song Mood Indigo
unforgettable dragging rhythm
        his smile
           the tie
              the stick pin
enter the dancer
in tights
        darkest blue
she dances sinuously
                right up to him
        the elegant smiling Duke
and the stickpin
              three-dimensional
she lies back upon
   it
     and revolves
             sexy, I so young
and the rhythm
           dragged out
enter the man in black
is he her fate?
          a dangerous destiny
  O infamous race riots
  of Washington D.C.!
slowly they revolve
            is she dying?
            she is dying slowly

and the Duke
the audience so still
          so rapt
Saturday matinees of vaudeville
     my childhood
already in love today
          perhaps
they have left the stage
          and she returns
        somehow a different
              dancer
    and on the tie pin
          she lies back
as the curtain descends
          on a strange love affair
on the afternoon
       I first heard
         Mood Indigo
everyone claps
       the curtains
          close
farewell! dancing madness
         we will meet again
     in Harlem

Rain

quilts the pond and
out from under its plumped-upness
a snapping turtle
pokes its head and
munches a morsel of water-lily leaf.
The sky
falls down in bits and pieces.
Does the face
of the pond
show the level of the water table?
Mebbe yes,
mebbe no.
A girl
no,
an ironwood tree
stands there
so young, so sinewy and slim
as though soft-water rinses were
all it ever wanted.
A branch
heavily shifts
its leaves.
Something —
a frog?—
goes plop.
The rough-cut grass,
stuck randomly
with flowers,
accepts the world's shampoo.

Birds

Little Portion
Tuesday, May 10, 1988

start up in gray,
in moist green,
branches laid
across, one call
a ratchet, and
"cooo-cooo,"
a silver spike
thin as a hypodermic
needle: "Just
a little stick."

A congeries of what
once were muddy lanes
shooting, one
into another,
randomly, tangled
as twigs. A round

bed of peonies,
hard in bud,
dark of leaf
and wet, wet:
Long Island Sound
so near, not quite
out of sight.

The birds stop.
The Post Road
shines mutedly,
an asphalt river.
The busy cars
begin to go about
their business.

Time, here, at
Little Portion,
for morning prayer.
Birds join in,
the bell at
the Poor Clares'
convent clangs,
a mourning dove
persists. Soft

morning green
(the longer one
lives, the more
to forget),
budded shapes
of branches
interlaced:
three grays,
sky, road, path.

Shadowy Room

for Brother Thomas Carey
June 27, 1988

". . . tall buildings swayed
in downtown San Francisco.
No reports
    of injuries
        at present."
Perishable perfection
of Glenn Gould playing
Bach purls on, oblivious
of interruption, building
course on
course, harmonious
in all lights,
all weathers, not unlike
la Rotonda and
so much airier,
spider webs and skeletons
of leaves,
the contiguity
of panes of glass. "No
reports
of injuries at present:
details later."
Mortal music, leading,
leading on,
to San Francisco,
the Golden Gate,
the hands of God.

White Boat, Blue Boat

for Hy Weitzen

Two boats parked
and posing in
the sun-struck
winter landscape:
rough grass, bare
with green washes.
Against self-colored
bark, lithe twigs
end in red buds:
you can't see it,
the red, and when
you do, you can't
not see it, against
a scaling trunk that,
higher than three
men on each
other's shoulders,
becomes more trunks.
Beyond, marsh grass
and reeds scratched
swiftly in.
A woman goes by,
her dog, too,
in short lopes:
a mutt. The day
can't get brighter,
clearer, but it
brightens, brightens,
so much and so
much more under
infinite cloudlessness
and icy spaces
and endless mystery.

Over the hills

the Jersey hills
to grandfather's house
and mother's and father's
(yours, not mine)
and that Morristown cemetery
where they lie
—well, not father:
instantly,
the complexity
of family history
no matter how simple-seeming,
how forthright. A nice,
really a nice
cemetery: rolling somewhat,
like the small clouds
in all the February blue,
and stuck
with admirable trees
and well kept up,
not offensively spruce:
plenty of dead leaves
scurrying about. Few
Roman bank-type
mausoleums. Beckers
abound, and other German names
among the Smiths, the Mellons,
 the Courtneys. Your mother called
on her marker,
as she was in life, Sallie:
she hated Sarah Loraine.
A beautiful woman
with a rough side to her tongue,
who always turned
to her father in troublesome times,

and here he is again. When
the other father (yours)
went off to war
he said, "Now you
must take care
of mother." A lot
to lay on a three-year-old!
Of course
he came home,
of course
you were jealous, and
like nearly all
the brokers in Far Hills
he drank.
Oh boy did he drink.
O well,
didn't we all? Life
can be cruel, and
tormented your mother with
one of its cruelest ailments,
long drawn out,
grinding.
But you still were young
and she well
when she took you to see
that Broadway hit whose star
she had such a crush on.
You sat together
in a box by the stage.
The show went on
until
(*and then? and then?*)
Pinza
looked up at Sallie
and sang,
"Some enchanted evening . . ."

A cardinal

in the branches of
the great plane tree
whistles its song:

or is it that mimic
Fairfield
saluting the day

under the branches of
his great plane tree
in his springtime yard?

Ajaccio Violets

Showered, shaved, splashed
(Ajaccio Violets) I
at first light
On Sunday morning go
out to get the *Times* and
by the elevator
two girls and a boy
passing a joint:
I
say good morning and
they
look up sullen-eyed and
don't say squat

The vapors of a humid day
and mountainous turds
of black-bagged garbage and
up the street
he comes: the house drunk
too heavily ballasted to leeward
by the *Sunday Times*:

he
ships water, rights himself,
veers past
the harbor buoy
and somehow makes it, maybe:
will he waken
late in the day
and find it, the *Sunday Times*,
that weighty testimonial to
conspicuous consumption,
scattered
beside the bed, unread,
half-read, unreadable
with that head
and those eyes,
those eyes?

Shaker

There was simply
nothing to look at:
a white empty room
with pegs to hang
chairs on: you know

the kind that I mean
the kind that look
like the way that
                    the way that

Teddy Wilson
plays the piano: each
note is so clear

I pointed
the camera down
the hall:
"An Arrangement in White":

the door of the closet
ajar: the lid of
one seat was up:
straight lines:
no curves.

There was a shop: pot
holders, a big bag
of apples: crisp, sharp.

I looked back
at the girl who looked
back
at me: perhaps to be
the last Shaker
at Sabbathday Lake.

Three Gardens

4404 Stanford

On the steep slope by the drive he
built a rock garden: each
different, from schist
to granite to
you name it, sort of a giant hunk
of conglomerate, of
which there was a hunk, purplish,
with bits of crap
caught up in it. Sedum,
maybe some moss pinks:
it was a *rock* garden,
a garden of rocks, but not
Kyoto style.

Erta Canina

Any place else it
was just a yard: but
if it's in Florence,
up above Florence, with some pots
of this-a and that-a
and a giantly ancient cypress
of dark and towering smoke, shut
in on itself, then
it's a garden. One night (in bed,
not yet asleep) from the boughs
of the cypress, a sound
so strange, so old, so new, so piercing
and steady, so clear, so loud (moonlight
in bright bars on the brick floor)
that, yes, of course,
at last:
the nightingale.

Chelsea

Petunias, this year,
got the gate and in
the window box that sits
on my balcony, are
three stout plants
of dianthus of an uncertain sort:
two rosy ones
and another a dark, smouldering,
passionate red. They
are more or less at center: in
front, demurely shiny,
green-leaved basil:
at the corners,
sage and rosemary. Drawn by the sun,
woven by the wind, they
intermingle: the herbs flower
unexpectedly with rose-red lights.
Behind,
up the 1880s iron balustrade, twine
a few implacable thin tendrils
of morning glory.

Let's All hear It For Mildred Bailey!

The men's can at Café Society Uptown
was need I say it? Upstairs
and as I headed for the stairs I
stumbled slightly
not about to fall
and Mildred Bailey
swept by in a nifty outfit:
off-brown velvet
but in a simple suit-effect
studded with brass nail heads
(her hair dressed with stark simplicity)
"Take it easy, Sonny," she
advised me and passed on to the supper club
(surely no supper was
served at Café you-know-which?)
A star spoke to me
in person! No one
less than Mildred Bailey!

Downstairs I nursed one drink
(cheap is cheap)
and Mildred Bailey got it on
and the boys all stood and shouted
"Mama Won't You Scrap Your Fat?"
a lively number
during the brownout
in war-haunted, death-smeared
NY

Then things got better, greater:
Mildred Bailey sang immortal hits
indelibly
permanently
marked by that voice
with built-in laughter
perfect attack: always
on the note
not behind or above it
and the extra something nice
that was that voice
a quality, a sound she had
on a disc, a waxing
you know it: Mildred Bailey

The night progressed:
a second drunk–oops–drink
(over there, boys, in what seemed
like silence boxcars rolled on
loaded with Jews, gypsies, nameless
forever others: The Final Solution
a dream of
Adolf Hitler:
Satan incarnate)

Mildred Bailey winds up the show
with a bouncy
number: when she gets back
to Brooklyn
from cheapo cruise ship
visitation:
Havana, Cuba
(then the door stood wide
to assorted thrills)
the next one in her life
ain't gonna be no loser, a clerk
oh no
"You can bet that he'll be Latin"

And Mildred Bailey, not
quite alone
in her upstate farmhouse
the rain is falling
she listens to another voice
somehow sadly
it is singing a song:
music
in a world gone wrong

Noon Office

A snowy curtain
slides up the sky.
Across the road,
dead trees whose
tops a hurricane
snapped off, rise
straight and pallid
out of green honey-
suckle nests. That
big tree, nearest
the house, goes
leathery, elephantine,
stands
on one leg.
The blessing—
the bliss—
of one afternoon:
an infestation
of silence. May God
forgive us. To no
one's memory we
erect dead trees.

Simone Signoret

Look, Mitterrand baby, your telegram
of condolence to Yves
Montand tells it like it is
but just once can't some high
placed Frenchman forget about the
gloire de France while the world
stands still a moment and all
voices rise in mourning
a star of stars:
Simone Signoret was and is
immortal
(thanks to seeming permanence
yes the silver screen? *l'écran?*)
Simone Signoret, A. K. A.
Mme. Yves Montand, is dead: Let's
re-read Tennyson's "Ode
to the Duke of Wellington"
with subtle emendations:
after all Simone never brought
about deaths by zillions on
a battlefield: no simply adult
entertainment as ambiguous
women beginning
with *Dédée d'Anvers*: Dédée
mixes with the wrong type
waterfront layabouts in
Antwerp and of course
she became some sort of
"star overnight" so let's for-
get about Academy Award
winner *Room at the Top* and
turn full attention to
Casque d'Or meaning

"Golden Helmet" and here
in this still in today's
Times she is wearing
her golden helmet of hair
and musing on the strange
destiny that right at the be-
ginning she does a circular
dance with her soon-to-be
lover (one arm behind back
one arm hangs straight down)
and he's a carpenter (we
find out all about that) and
utterly evil Claude Dauphin
and at the end she watches
from a window his execution—
friend lover, that is, not
well-disposed-of Dauphin—
and she, staring and staring
implacably staring, woman
with mysterious eyes, under
a smooth brushed helmet
of golden hair: I always
remember you like that
and we used to quaff
liquid refreshments in
the same midtown Parisian
bar (Christ, that was long
ago) and I wondered who
the hell is this Simone
Signoret
and what's so great about
Deédée d'Anvers (I still
haven't seen it): Simone
(may I call you Simone

just this once?) tonight
one star in the real sky
the starry firmament
goes out and the rest
the stars, the stars!
shine more brightly for
that star of stars
with almond-eyes
and a well-brushed
helmet of golden hair
and I truly miss you
Simone Signoret

The light within

and the light without: the shade
of a rainy April morning:
subtle shadows
cast backward by lamplight
upon daylight,
soft unforceful daylight,
the essence
of cloud cover
descending mistily into the street:
and the unwhitely
white surround of a curling photograph
models itself
as north light
modeled the face in the photograph:

and against a window
a tree shows
each lightly tinted leaf
another shadowy shade, some
transparently, some
not: and, in the corner
the dark bisected
by the light that falls
from without (created
by its absence)
lies luminous within itself:
the luminous dark within.

Advent

Open my eyes on the welcome
rosy shock of sunshine.

Open the first little door
of my Advent calendar:

a darling hobby horse
on wheels. Open

the window a crack: and
quickly close it against

a knife-like draught. The day
looks warmer than it is.

Six something

on June 5th, '90:
closed shops
and well-washed
bluelessness, and
across the street
a man finishes
his polishing. I
count seedlings:
always counting,
cars, trees, not
infinitudes of
leaves. The Veterans
Building hides all
the Empire State Building
excepting
its antennae
rising in stages
first woven then
slim out of thick
to an ultimate
needle taper pricking
the day: its
point a test
of clarity. And
where is God
in all this?
Asleep? Resting?
and if so, from
what? Eternity
is tireless
surely, like:
rest now forever
blessed tired heart,
wakening otherwhere
in bell-like blue.

Andrew Lord Poems

the flattened shape
the first shape
a bowl

a jug   a vase   a dish

rectangles   cones

lustre glaze
crazed

a fine craze
                    hidden
almost
                    maple keys
among maple leaves

plunged
hot in water
Chinese ink
rubbed in

——

when is a funerary vase
not funerary?
a vase not a vase?

the shapes of things

tea pot ceramic
vase of bronze vase

trumpet flare
beaker
gu

touching and holding

pressing and holding

———

a random arrangement
changing within itself

      33 pieces   modelling

black
black
      not black
      Wedgwood obsidian
slate
darkening toward black

16 pieces   copper

blue   copper and tin

16 pieces   copper

red   copper and tin
      rouge flambé

———

where light falls
where shade falls
      pressing
      pulling

drunken tea pot
slope-shouldered urn
beauty
of oddity

stoneware clay
matte finish

when is a glaze
not a glaze?

fired
not hot enough
    no silica
    no glass-
    iness
    no shine
flat
matte

———

coiled clay
joined
in three
parts

pretty
       breakable

pretty
       fragile

Sèvres   Meissen

touching and holding

modelling
       hand marks

a knife
     a rolling
pin

———

geometry

age 16
working
with clay
      ceramics

cubist
or
geometric
or
constructivist
angled geometry

1 year
in factory
in Delft

excited
about glazes now
very involved in glazes

finest crackle
see it
hear it

an algebra
of the stars

——

packing up
funeral feast
dishes

wrapping dishes

sending dishes

a platter
shaped
like a peanut

38

gold drip
on vessel lip

a cup   a basin

fracture
and
      durability
a trivet

———

always
a shape
  in mind
changes
  each time

freedom
breeds control

elegant
     notebooks

       a handle
twists
    back on itself

dark
    runnels
    over crazing
unwiped
dribbles

———

dead-leaf
    tea set

39

knobbly
  dirtied
  by gold

indescribable
  colors
    of fired

metal
favrile
lustrousness

  golden copper
coming forward
 darker
manganese
 coming forward

uncontrollable
           fire
whichever
  it chooses
  to be

———

most beautiful
  glazes
deadliest
  ingredients

lead
manganese dioxide
silver nitrate
copper oxide
tin oxide

glazes with
    darkness

40

boding through
lights
on the unsmoothedness
bulky
askew

a bowl
with thumb
   drawn lines
another bowl ·
      marked
      by thumb nail

here
gold
tries
to come through

Under the Hanger

from Gilbert White's Journals

Wood lark whistles. Hogs carry straw.
Sky lark sings.
Young cucumber swells.
Frogs croak: spawn abounds.
Cold & black. Harsh, hazy day.
Backward apples begin to blow.
Frost, sun, fog, rain, snow. Bunting twitters.
No dew, rain, rain, rain.
Swans flounce & dive.
Chilly & dark.
Dark and spitting. Indian flowers in Dec'r!
Ground very wet. The nightingale sings.
Blackcap sings. The sedge-bird a delicate polyglott.
The titlark begins to sing: a sweet songster!
Turtle coos.
Asparagus begins to sprout.
Cuckoo cries.
No house-martins appear.

Apricots, peaches, & nectarines swell:
sprinkled trees with water, & watered the roots.
Oaks are felled: the bark runs freely.
The leaves of the mulberry trees hardly begin to peep.
Showers, sun & clouds, brisky air.
Much hay spoiled: much not cut.

Put meadow hay in large cock.
Hay well made at last.
Sun, sweet day.

All things in a drowning condition!

First day of winter. Snow on the ground.
Gathered in all the grapes. Snow on the hills.
Full moon.
Rooks resort to their nest-trees.
Grey & sharp.
Earth-worms lie out & copulate.
Great rain. Hops sadly washed.
Ice bears: boys slide.

Rain, rain, rain.

The road in a most dusty, smothering condition.
Full moon. My well is shallow & the water foul.
The grass burns.
A plant of missle-toe grows on a bough of the medlar.
The air is full of insects.
Turkies strut and gobble.
Snow wastes: eaves drip. Cocks crow.
Sun, bright & pleasant.
The boys are playing in their shirts.
Bees thrive. Asparagus abounds.
Dark & chilly, rain. Cold & comfortless.
Mossed the white cucumber bed.
Snow covers the ground.

Planted 12 goose-berry trees, & three monthly roses,
        & three Provence roses.
The voice of the cockow is heard in the hanger.
Grass lamb.
Grey, sprinkling, gleams with thunder.
Wavy, curdled clouds, like the remains of thunder.

Pease are hacked: rye is reaping: turnips thrive &
    are hoing.
Stifling dust.
Sweet moonshine.
Boys slide on the ice!

Dew, bright, showers: thunder, gleam of sun.
Straw-berries, scarlet, cryed about.
Straw-berries dry, & tasteless.
Taw & hop-scotch come in fashion among the boys.
The sun mounts and looks down on the hanger.
Crown Imperials blow, & stink.
Much gossamer.
Moles work, & heave up their hillocks.
Ice within doors.
Rime.
Snow on the ground.
Snow in the night: snow five inches deep.
Snow on the ground.
Icicles hang in eaves all day.
Snow lies on the hill.

Crocus's make a gaudy show.
Cuculus cuculat: the voice of the cuckoo is heard in
    Blackmoor woods.
The air is filled with floating willow-down.
Fog, sun, pleasant showers, moonshine.
Here & there a wasp.
Black-birds feed on the elder-berries.
Frost, ice, sun pleasant moon-light.
Frost, ice, bright, red even, prodigious white dew.
Thunder, lightening, rain, snow!

Vast damage in various parts!
No frost.
Daffodil blows.

Daffodil blows.
Sweet weather. Mackerel.
Soft wind. The woodpecker laughs.
Cinnamon-roses blow.
Flowers smell well this evening: some dew.
The distant hills look very blue.

Clouds, hail, shower, gleams.
Sharp air, & fire in the parlor.
Sweet day, golden even, red horizon.
Snow-drops, & crocus's shoot.
Vast frost-work on the windows.
Longest day: a cold, harsh solstice

Thunder & hail.
Yellow evening.
Potatoes blossom.
Men cut their meadows.
Goose-berries wither on the trees.
The seeds of the lime begin to fall.
Grey, & mild, gleams.
Grey, sun, pleasant, yellow even.
Dark & wet.
Rain, rain, gleams. Venus resplendent.
Showers of hail, sleet. Gleams.
The Cuckoo is heard on Greatham common.

Cut the first cucumber.
Pulled the first radish.
Early orange-lilies blow.
Cut *five* cucumbers.
Bright, sun, golden even.
Cut *eight* cucumbers.
Provence roses blow against a wall.
Cut *ten* cucumbers.
Dames violets very fine.

Men wash their sheep.

Yellow Flowers

for William Corbett

Pie-wedge petals
deeply pinked and
the yellow of yellow oranges,
set in a single
layer, ray out
from a pollen shedding tuft:
see the bright dust
on this filing cabinet
enameled the greeny-cream
of the seed-cradling inner flesh
of an avocado
               these yellow flowers
on wiry stems, bunched
in a thick gray pitcher:
two bands of washed-out blue,
two transfers in same ("You
don't want
that clunky thing")

and petals fall and tufts
puff up, a brown fuzz ball
with a green frill: the hard
green balls with green frills
of course are buds: and

you plunge your face
in their massed
papery powdery sweetness
and grunt in delight
at their sunset sweetness

it begins with C

yes: coreopsis

Blossoming Oakwood

dead-ends at 19th one
block over from Dolores
(more magisterial, more
of a street
of a street), its houses
not so much quake
resistant as egg crate
concessions to
the possibility of one:
crumple and build again
under the colorlessness
of thickened
Pacific moistened air:
draw in cold breaths
if you can. On Oakwood,
run down, kept up, tinted
San Francisco style,
on Ash Wednesday (early
in February
this year), geraniums—
coarse, weedy, pink—
make a hedge where
there's no room to grow.
One front yard
a delirious garden
jumble sale: a bush
like a sponge
with a myriad small leaves,
jostles a camellia
(blood red, rain fades
a washy orange). Across
a petty scramble
of undergrowth along

an overgrown path,
a window-blocking banana
shredding, thriving, and
trashy, trashy, tropics trashy,
urgent, jubilant, thrashing
on Oakwood Street, on
Ash Wednesday, the day
death begins, and life.

A Chapel

small, just
a room,
the altar
at center,
one wall
all glass,
out in
wet twilight:
by a fence
a tall clump
of calla lilies
(*Zantedeschia aethiopica*
roadside weeds
of Ethiopia),
a camellia
two stories tall,
in full bloom:
they fall
whole and
lie like cow flops
on the grass.
Outdoor stairs:
San Francisco.
". . . and to dust
you shall return"
he imposes
the ashes.

A View

Little Portion
Tuesday, May 10, 1988

How come a thickish tree
casts so thin a shadow
and that sign-supporting pipe
none at all? (here comes Tom)

The road dries off, lighter
and lighter (there goes
Tom, in the red car, after
flour). In the further

distance, a baby-blue camper,
after reeds and dead tree trunks,
peeled and weathered,
and the creosoted phone poles

Closer, on grass, the sunlight
breathes: fades and brightens,
brightens and fades, sparkles
yellow–green on green

Out of nowhere, a breeze
tosses the junk (soon
to be leaves) on twig ends.
Here comes Charlie, the cat.

Closer, window screen and
a six-light window sash
pushed part way up another
makes a fifteen-light window

framed by thick white net.
Closer, a bag says, The Cellar.
Closer, a pair of slippers, and
(khaki canvas) a Maine hiking shoe

invites my foot to go
out there, into the view
of May 10th, 1988
                    Here

comes Tom (he
got the flour) and there
sits Charlie, a white
cat on a green hummock.

This soft October

Monday, October 17, 1988

           mid-morning
the light, what light
             there is
that is, comes
from the east
          under the sky
not from it
        more a pulsation
than a glow
           the glow
that on Sunday
           (only
yesterday? was
            it only yesterday?
It was
     it was) shone
from the west
          from
Manhattan
        the train throbbed
on toward
       light tasting
of Chateau Yquem or
            less grand
more glorious
        the fortified wine
used at the
      sacrament
in communion
       this is the cup
of life
      the blood
of salvation
        light lighting up
the scrub
      in red
and purple
      and gold

On the dresser

that had a swivel
mirror, a swivel
picture frame: greenish-
silvery-grayish:
in it
a photograph (silvery-
grayish) of
a girl, a young
woman: large
soft eyes, hair swept
 around her head
and forehead, a filmy
dress over a
silken dress with an
embroidered bodice
flounce. Next
to it,
a matching
(greenish-silvery-grayish)
bud vase
in which once I
put a stem
of freesia: Bernie
liked that
fragrant tribute to
the beautiful
beautiful mother he
never knew. Time
passed and at
the draft board physical

a doctor said, "Wasn't
your mother Hortense
Chittenden? I
used to dance
with her. Now,
then, she died. . ."
"...of influenza,"
Bernie said. The doctor
frowned, looked
down at the form and
wrote,
"in childbirth."

Princess Di

Intricacies of a devious mind
run amok are explicable
to me who cannot explain:
Helena, you came bravely
into a room I knew was bugged
(outside in the hall
peered and lingered
a literal murderer disguised
as a black man ready to bring
me the ultimate message:
my death:) and bold as brass
but so much prettier in
you came with a flower
wrapped, concealed in
paper and I tried to converse
in the language of the dance:
slipping fingers on fingers
meaning rings, meaning jewels
and the inside of the paper
was white and blank you
laughed to see it and I
saw a message from Korea
holy, mysterious as a stone
a white stone to hold
in hand and meditate to
pray and you smiled and
you left a soft pink rose
on my bed and I went
back of beyond to
the place so far away
where time is eternal and
infinity is grasped not
understood: and when I
came round there was the rose
in a clear plastic container
aslant the petals not yet

curling back and I knew that
the rose was extra special
and you came and I asked
"Who gave me that rose?" You
laughed and you said, "Why
I did: its name is
Princess Di" and each day
as I lay and time slowed
down to its usual shuffle
I watched as the petals
curled back and
came to a point I
exclaimed to myself, "That
point is unique: this
softer, smaller rose
is the hybridized offspring
of Georg Arends!"
silvery, pink
larger with sharply
pointed petals, the only
rose to do so (I thought,
I imagined) what joy
to see it recur in Princess
Di named for we all know
who and the Chinese lady
heard what I said when
she asked and she said,
"Princess Diana the Princess
Diana" and as the days
passed and you came
to escort me home and
the rose I had watched
grown fat and soft
expired as I left
and I thought, "Beautiful
Princess. farewell!"

Haze

hangs heavy
down into trees: dawn
doesn't break today,
the morning
seeps into being, one
bird, maybe
two, chipping
away at it. A white dahlia,
big
as Baby Bumstead's head,
leans
its folded petals
at a window, a lesson
in origami
Frantically, God
knows what
machine: oh no,
just Maggio's
garbage truck.
Staring
at all the roughage
that hides an estuary,
such urbanity
seems inapt: the endless city
builds on and on
thinning out, here and there,
for the wet green velvet towels
("slight imperfections")
of summer
("moderately priced")
and a hazy morning
in August,
even that
we may grow to love.

James Schuyler - Last Poems

An afterword by Lee Harwood.

Growing in front of me this October morning in a white ceramic pot on the scrubbed wood table is a phalaenopsis orchid with an arc of flowers. The white fleshy petals surround a crimson mouth and tongue and, deeper inside, a crimson striped throat. The white seems the whitest of whites, yet a very faint pink blush soaks through from the back of the petals. They're amazing and beautiful and stop you in your tracks as you enter the room. Just as finding wild orchids like the near unbelievable bee orchid or the burnt orchid amongst the grass of a hillside or clifftop literally stops you in your tracks. James Schuyler well knew this commonly shared joy, relished it, even though his big love was garden flowers and, most of all, roses. His long poem here *Horse-Chestnut Trees and Roses* is a very catalogue of roses.

"At the corner of the house Rosa Mutabilis fluttered
its single, changeable wings. My favorite, perhaps.

Then, in the border, along the south side of
the white house, Golden Wings (a patented rose —
did you know you can patent roses? Well you can);
prickly, purplish Rose de Rescht; ...
Mabel Morrison, lifting her blowsy white blooms
to the living-room windows.

Then Georg Arends, whose silver-pink petals
uniquely fold into sharp points (or is Georg
my favorite?)."

Even the painfully clear hospital poem is titled after a rose named *Princess Di.*

"and you came and I asked
"Who gave you that rose" You
laughed and you said, "Why
I did: its name is

Princess Di" and each day
as I lay and time slowed
down to its usual shuffle
I watched as the petals
curled back and
came to a point I
exclaimed to myself, "That
point is unique: this
softer, smaller rose
is the hybridized offspring
of Georg Arends!"

Like the naturalists such as Gilbert White and Richard Jeffries and gardeners like William Robinson that he so admired, James Schuyler knew how to look. He knew how such precise and unprejudiced attention brought infinite delight and wonder. In one of Gilbert White's letters to Thomas Pennant, White writes - "It is I find in zoology as it is in botany: all nature is so full that that district produces the greatest variety which is the most examined." (8 October 1768). This care and patience and good humour were a way of life both for White and Schuyler. The rewards were so obvious to them - and not just in matters of natural history. As is found in his Diary his understanding came from specific things rather than generalities. He was in this what might truly be called a painterly poet. His poem *White Boat, Blue Boat* ends with -

"...The day
can't get brighter,
clearer, but it
brightens, brightens,
so much and so
much more under
infinite cloudlessness
and icy spaces
and endless mystery."

Schuyler was bemused and fascinated by the world. Whether it was the "icy spaces" or "rain quilts the pond" *(Rain)* or describing the play of light on "a rainy April morning" in *The Light Within*, he looked and relished what he saw and the words he chose to describe what he saw. As he wrote more directly in the title poem of his earlier book *A Few Days* -

> "Let's love today, the what we have now, this day, not
>   today or tomorrow or
> yesterday, but this passing moment, that will
>   not come again."

It follows naturally from this that a reader of Schuyler's poems nearly always finds himself or herself in the present. Not a narrow present, but one that includes asides, memories, double-takes, and all the vivid associations that pour into the brain in a few minutes. Reading one of James Schuyler's poems often feels like looking over his shoulder as he writes. The process is that open to view. In fact the "process" is very much part of the poem. It's akin to listening to Glen Gould playing Bach's *Goldberg Variations* (and Beethoven's piano sonatas too). The way Gould tentatively plays the notes, searching his way through the music, as though recreating Bach's thinking and progress as Bach builds a piece. As though making it up as he goes along. It could go this way? or that? no, this way. In his poem *Shadowy Room* Schuyler touchs on this.

> "Perishable perfection
> of Glenn Gould playing
> Bach purls on, oblivious
> of interruption, building
> course on
> course, harmonious
> in all lights,
> all weathers,..."

So many of his poems have this lovely quality where we watch the poem unroll and build as we read. Poems like *Rain* and *Over the Hills* and *Horse-Chestnut Trees and Roses*. And behind this apparent openness and spontaneity is his great artistry in being able to create such events, to create such "fictions".

What I love in these poems, beside his exact eye and perfect ear, are the stories these "fictions" tell us. Schuyler writes with wit and self-mockery, with a relish for language worthy of Ronald Firbank. He plays with us as he stops and starts and goes off on digressions while he lets loose his story. Whether it be, in *Over the Hills*, the story-teller's trick of pulling in his audience -

> "The show went on
> until
> (*and then? and then?*)
> Pinza
> looked up at Sallie
> and sang,
> 'Some enchanted evening...'"

Or to remind us that meanwhile other things are happening at the same time in the world outside the immediate story, as he does in *Let's all hear it for Mildred Bailey!*.

> "(Over there, boys, in what seemed
> like silence boxcars rolled on
> loaded with Jews, gypsies, nameless
> forever others:..."

In the Mildred Bailey poem, like Frank O'Hara's poem *The Day Lady Died* in memory of Billie Holiday, the poem builds up a list of "daily details" then finally swoops off beyond the immediate moments. The fiction may be presented as what O'Hara called an "I do this I do that" poem, may even read like a journal where daily life and the poem appear the same. Schuyler's days in the country or in New York City at the Chelsea Hotel. But it's a finely tuned artifice and comes from a long tradition of such artifice. There's obviously the influence of his friends like Frank O'Hara and John Ashbery and younger contemporaries like the poet and painter Joe Brainard. But, going back further - as he said in interviews - there's the great influence of Arthur Waley's Chinese translations. The example of poems that are clear and elegant and seemingly direct and simple. Poems where the poet is not an isolated heroic figure but a social creature enjoying or enduring the "ordinary" experiences of life. He talks with us, doesn't harangue us.

The other strong influence was Elizabeth Bishop, a poet of an earlier generation but one he admired immensely, and who in turn valued his poems. Her poem *The Moose* for example is a marvellous poem in every way and you can see in it why Schuyler so prized her work. The poem talks of the equal marvel we feel when faced with the natural world in all its forms. Written in a quiet and clear undramatic voice, it details a bus journey from Great Village, Nova Scotia, south to Boston. The landscapes, the small towns and villages passed through ("where a woman shakes a tablecloth / out after supper"), the passengers' conversations, and the sudden appearance of the moose in the bus's headlights standing calmly in the middle of the moonlit road. In a way it's an "ordinary" though special, even magical, occurence, but one that somehow lifts us so far beyond the poem. Even beyond the miracle of the moose! (No offense to the moose intended, of course.)

Schuyler may have a "low keyed conversational tone", to quote from Ashbery's obituary for him in *The Independent*. He may be more relaxed in style and certainly more confessional than Bishop. But it's the same essence there that drove Elizabeth Bishop to write her poem and, I'm guessing here, Po Chu-i to write his poems and Schuyler in turn to write his own poems.

That James Schuyler's *Last Poems* should be first published as a book here in Britain is a nice exchange, an appropriate gift from a poet who was steeped in British literature. He was an American "Anglophile" who never visited this country. He read widely and voraciously. 18th and 19th and early 20th century volumes of letters, diaries, books on gardening, books on the countryside, novels and poetry. William Cobbett's *Rural Rides*, Charles Darwin's writings, Francis Kilvert's

Diary, Virginia Woolf's letters, E.F.Benson's *Lucia* novels. And he regularly took *The Countryman* magazine. Need I say more? That this last book of Schuyler's should include a long poem that is a cut-up of Gilbert White's *Journals* seems therefore only right and appropriate. Always this leaning towards and love of the particular, the "small" daily details.

In Schuyler's 1972 collection *The Crystal Lithium* in a poem titled *Empathy and New Year* he writes -

"Got coffee and started
reading Darwin: so modest,
so innocent, so pleased at
the surprise that he
should grow up to be him."

In his *Diary* on 1st January 1968 he writes more fully. "Began the New Year reading Darwin's autobiography and letters - so modest and so delighted with his accomplishments. A little dumb, perhaps, ("The sight of a naked savage in his native land is an event which can never be forgotten.") but only in the gloriously innocent way of a man whose concerns are on the largest and most detailed scale." This could be a partial summary of James Schuyler himself, though maybe his "dumbness" taking other forms.

October 1998
Brighton & Hove, Sussex.